# Along Life's Highway

# Along Life's Highway

by
Clarence Edward Macartney

Compiled and Edited by Harry E. Farra

BAKER BOOK HOUSE
Grand Rapids, Michigan

Library of Congress Catalog Card Number: 75-97726

Copyright, 1969, by
Baker Book House Company

PHOTOLITHOPRINTED BY CUSHING - MALLOY, INC.
ANN ARBOR, MICHIGAN, UNITED STATES OF AMERICA
1969

Lincoln Christian College

## Acknowledgments

The materials in this volume were selected from the Macartney Collection of Geneva College and used by their kind permission.

Gratitude is also due to Dr. Macartney's former secretary, Mrs. Tabler, for her help in filling in details that had obscured themselves since Dr. Macartney's passing in 1957. The volume, as well, reflects the saving hand of my typist, Mrs. Rhodes.

I know that Dr. Macartney would want this volume dedicated to his three great churches and the company of prophets that have taken his place.

What part I've had in the collecting and editing of this volume I dedicate to my wife, Vonnie, for her own dedication to my task.

Harry E. Farra

Geneva College
Beaver Falls, Pennsylvania

44885

# Contents

# 1

## Travel at Your Own Risk

*"Everyone of us shall give account of himself to God."*
— Romans 12:26

On a long automobile trip one summer, I amused myself with reading the highway signs. They were always in conspicuous places, printed in large characters, and easily read as the car flashed by. The highway commissioners had put up these signs for the convenience and guidance and warning of all who travelled along the road. The signs represented the collected wisdom and experience of those who had travelled the roads and were familiar with them. Reading these signs, I fell to thinking of the great highway of life which we all travel, and thus lifted into a higher meaning some of those roadway signs which I saw. These signs came to stand for certain fundamental truths and principles of life.

One sign which I read frequently was this — "Travel at your own risk." Sometimes it was introduced by another statement — "Road under construction," or "Bridge condemned." By posting these signs the commissioners not only warned the traveller to be cautious and careful, but absolved the county or state of responsibility in case of accident on that part of the road so designated. If the traveler came to harm on the road, he could bring no suit for damages. He was travelling at his own risk.

## I. YOUR RESPONSIBILITY

"Travel at your own risk." In the long journey of life which we are all taking, every man travels at his own risk. You are the responsible party. Your friends, your neighbor, your parents, the community in which you live, your schools, your teachers, your relatives, are not the responsible ones, but you yourself. You do the travelling and you incur the risks, whatever they are. Another proverb expresses this in familiar language, "Every man has his own life to live."

The very beginning of the race shows that every man travels at his own risk, and that man is an accountable and responsible creature. He was placed in a garden where everything was fair and favorable, and where he was, nevertheless, free and responsible, and had to take the risks of a forbidden tree. If he ate of this, sorrow and suffering were sure to follow. This is always true of the Garden of Life. It has its prohibitions, restrictions, and dangers. Life is great, but it has great risks and solemn responsibilities of which no man can divest himself. Some speak of life as a game where we play opposite an invisible opponent who checkmates us at our slightest blunder. Others have thought of life as a battle field where every man must fight his own battle. There is no discharge from this warfare which is appointed unto man. When King Ahab was commanded to give battle to the Syrians, he inquired, "Who shall command the battle?" The answer of the prophet was, "Thou!" That is a word God's prophet speaks to every one of us. The battle is ours. We alone can command it. If we fail in this battle, the only one to blame is ourselves.

## II. EVADING RESPONSIBILITY

Many attempts are made today to relieve men of responsibility, and along life's highway many false signs are posted telling the traveller that he travels, not at his own, but at another's risk. Some have tried to relieve man of responsibility on the ground of heredity, that the invisible hand of yesterday, of the generations back of him, have pushed him along the road of his transgression. Others have tried to persuade us that our environment is the responsible party, and that what we are and what we do is the inevitable result of our surroundings. There is truth in heredity, and truth in environment. But neither one absolves man of his own individual responsibility. "The soul that sinneth, it shall die." Each life is a universe to itself, and when we attempt to acquit ourselves on the ground that we act only according to the pressure of heredity or society, and that temptation was too strong for us, conscience rules us out of court with its solemn and arresting and convicting, "Thou art the man!"

In the story of man's first journey and first disaster, the man blamed the woman; and, incidentally, blamed God, too; for he said, "The woman thou gavest to be with me, she gave me of the tree, and I did eat." When the Lord asked the woman, she blamed the serpent, saying, "The serpent beguiled me, and I did eat." How true to human nature, which always seeks to put its load of guilt on the shoulders of someone else! Yet none of those involved in this first transgression were relieved of responsibility or exempted from punishment.

I remember once going through the Eastern Penitentiary, and talking in the cells with a number of the prisoners. The strange thing was that not one of the men in prison acknowledged that he deserved to be there. Each one blamed someone else, or blamed circumstances, and felt himself not guilty of the crime of which he had been convicted. This is a trait of human nature which is writ large, both without and within the prison walls.

## III. THE MORAL LAW INEXORABLE

Another trait of human nature is to indulge the hope and expectation that the law of cause and effect, of reaping as we sow, of sin finding us out, of suffering for folly, of retribution for sin, of the recoil of the broken law, while true and operative in other circumstances and other lives, will for some reason suspend its operation in our own case. Few, indeed, would actually say that this was what they hoped or expected. But multitudes act as if that were their plan of life; as if they could beat the system by which the moral world is run, and for some reason be exempted from its solemn exactions and retributions. But it is the wish which is father to the thought. Sin not only infatuates and lures men on, but blinds their eyes so that they cannot see the angel and the sword of retribution, as gold-blinded Balaam of old could not see the obstructing and contending angel in his path. But the moral Law is no respecter of persons. Every man travels at his own risk and bears his own burden of responsibility.

Daniel Webster, once asked what was the greatest thought that had passed through that wonderful brain, answered "My accountability to God." Life is a great journey, with wonderful goals which flash through cloud and fog and mist their glorious invitations. But we must travel carefully and live as accountable to God. Not in the sense which Henley meant it, but in the high and solemn and scriptural sense, "I am the captain of my soul and the master of my fate." See to it that you command your battle well. Do not expect that anyone else can fight or pray or suffer for you. Make the man of today the friend, and not the foe, of the man of tomorrow.

When we come to deal with God, sincerity and truth are the gateway to His presence and His blessing. If you are conscious now of mistakes, acknowledge them frankly and take the full responsibility upon yourself. If there have been sins of passion, go like the demoniacs to Christ, who can cast out the devils and the unclean spirits. If it is the sin of spiritual deadness and dullness, be carried to Him as the paralytics were, and ask Him to lift you up and make you walk again. If it has been the sin of falsehood or dishonesty, go to Him as the woman with the spirit of infirmity did, and He will make you straight and true. If it has been the sin of hate and withered sympathies and affections, go to Him as did the man with the withered hand, and He will make the blood of love course through your veins again. If you have been blind to life's greatness and opportunities and sacred tenderness — and how blind we sometimes are — go to Him as did the two blind men, who cried, "Thou son of David, have mercy on us," and He will open your eyes that you may see.

I cannot answer for you, and you cannot answer for me in the day of judgment. But I must one day answer and give an account for the message which I, as a messenger of God, gave to you. This is the message, then, that I have given to you today. We shall all one day stand before the judgment seat of Christ to give our account. In that day I cannot answer for you. You cannot answer for me. But there is one who, if you put your faith and trust in Him, and rely not on your own righteousness, but on His righteousness, will answer for you, and whose answer God will accept. If you have put your trust and faith in Christ, then you can say, "I know whom I have believed, and am persuaded that he is able to keep that which I have committed unto him against that day."

**2**

# The Man Behind Can't
# Read Your Mind

*"None of us liveth to himself."* — Romans 14:7

These highway signs, as we shall see, are powerful and practical preachers. They get to the root of the matter in a few words. Here is one of their timely sermons, THE MAN BEHIND CAN'T READ YOUR MIND.

This is a sign which you see now and then as you roll along the highway. It reminds you that you are not the only man who is on the road, that there are others near enough to you, behind you, or at your side, who can be hindered, hurt, injured, and even destroyed by the way you drive. Some years ago I went to visit an old friend in the hospital at Denver. He was a distinguished missionary to China, home on furlough. With an elder of one of the churches of Denver he was on his way to speak at a meeting in Colorado Springs. Without any signal or warning, the car in front of him suddenly turned out. In the collision which ensued my friend was badly injured and had to lie in the hospital for many weeks. Indeed, although six years have passed, he has never fully recovered from his injuries.

What was the trouble? How did it happen? The man in

front turned out without letting the man behind know what he was going to do. And since the man behind could not read his mind, the wreck took place.

## I. NONE LIVES TO HIMSELF

In the great text which I have chosen, "None of us liveth to himself," St. Paul speaks of our responsibility for our conduct and our influence upon other lives. The particular matter that he had in mind was eating meat which had been offered at the altar in one of the pagan temples. That was where the common people got most of their meat. They bought the meat that had been offered as a sacrifice to one of the gods. There were Christian disciples who thought it was not right for a Christian to eat such meat. For himself, Paul says that it makes no difference to him whether the meat has been offered to an idol or not, for an idol is "nothing." But if his eating such meat will be an offense and a stumbling block to his brother Christians, then, Paul says he will "eat no meat while the world standeth." He is keenly sensitive to his influence upon other men and will take care that the influence which goes out from him shall be such as will bless and not hurt another life.

There is both a conscious and unconscious influence for good and for evil. It is, alas, true that there are those who deliberately seek to lead others astray. Satan, who fell from heaven, desires to see all others fall. That is the secret of his constant assault upon the souls of men. There are sinners who seek to entice others to sin, and the warning of the Book of Proverbs, "My son, if sinners entice thee, consent thou not," is always a timely one. But much of the influence which we exert in life is unconscious.

## II. THERE IS AN UNCONSCIOUS
## INFLUENCE FOR EVIL

One of the pastors of this church, Dr. William Paxton, once declined to receive into the membership of the church a young man who was engaged in the liquor business. The young man, who came of a brewer's family in New York, and had never thought of his business as anything but respectable, took great offense when Dr. Paxton informed him that he did not feel he could receive him as a member of the church. In an angry mood he told Dr. Paxton, as he left the manse, that he would never have anything to do with this or any other church. But as he was leaving, Dr. Paxton said to him, "I would advise you to follow your wagons around over the city and see where they go, and the influence they exert." He never expected to see the young man again. But some months afterwards he came again to the manse, apologized for the rudeness of his speech on the former occasion, and told Dr. Paxton that he had taken his advice and had followed his liquor wagons over the city. He had separated himself from it entirely, and now wished to be received as a member of the church.

Driving at night through an unknown territory, you will often follow the tail light of the car in front of you. Although the man in the car in front does not know it, he is acting as a guide and pacemaker for you. If he takes the wrong turn, or goes off the road, you follow him. So it is in life. There's a man behind who is following us and who is being guided in the right or the wrong way by us.

Some years ago there was a very popular book, *For Whom the Bell Tolls*. The title was taken from the Seventeenth Devotion of the English preacher and poet, John Donne. His idea in that passage was exactly that of St. Paul, that none of us liveth to himself; that if a fragment of soil is washed away from the continent, the whole continent is affected thereby; and when the bell of death tolls, it tolls for us all. John Donne in his later years, when he was so powerful a preacher, preaching, as Isaac Walton said of him, "like an angel out of the clouds," is said to have expressed deep regret and sorrow over some of the things that he had written in his earlier days, and which were calculated to sow the seeds of licentiousness and immorality in the lives of others. John Newton, author of some of the best loved and most-sung hymns of the hymn book, collaborator with William Cowper in the Olney Hymns, when he was a profane and wicked sailor at sea, had led a young shipmate in the wrong path. When he was converted and brought to Christ, John Newton made very earnest, but ineffectual, attempts to reclaim the youth that he had led astray. What greater and keener pang of remorse could there be than the consciousness that you have influenced a mortal soul in the wrong direction?

In the Christian life and in the church, if you are faithful and regular and consistent and prayerful, others will be helped by you. A well-known judge, who had long deferred decision, at length waited upon the minister of the church and told him he desired to confess his faith and unite with the church. The minister asked him if there was any particular sermon he had preached which had finally led him to make the decision for Christ. "No," the judge replied, "it was the life of a member of the church who lives next to me in our block."

On the other hand, an inconsistent and faithless life on the part of a Christian man may keep another out of the church. It ought not to be so, for we follow Christ and confess our faith in him, and not in one another. Nevertheless, an unworthy life on the part of a church member will sometimes keep another out. And not only an unworthy life, but a neglect on the part of one man to confess his faith in Christ and to come into the church may set a wrong example for someone else. Amos Kendall, famous postmaster of the United States, founder of the Pony Express, when he was over seventy years of age, stood up in his church in Washington and said he had a confession of faith to make. The startled congregation thought he was going to confess to some fraud or transgression; but what they heard him say was that he had thought he could be a good, moral man without confessing his faith and becoming a member of the church. But he had recently learned of a man who had followed his example, and had said to himself that if it wasn't necessary for Mr. Kendall to unite with the church, it was not necessary for him. This man, being weaker than Kendall, had fallen into sin and died a wretched death. Kendall's conscience smote him because of this, and he said he recalled at least twelve men who might have been Christians had it not been for his example.

When judgment was pronounced upon the man in the story of the Fall in the Book of Genesis, God said to Adam, "Cursed is the ground for thy sake." Here at the very fountain of the stream of history, when man is judged and punished for his disobedience, he is told that the ground is cursed for his sake, because of what he had done. Because of his disobedience the ground was cursed. "Thorns also and thistles shall it bring forth to thee." You and I still feel the effects of the first man's transgression.

### III. THERE IS ALSO THE UNCONSCIOUS INFLUENCE FOR GOOD

If there are those for whose sake, because of whom, the ground of life is cursed, thank God there are also those for whose sake, and because of whose example, life's ground is blessed. Here is an influence which cannot be checked or held back, any more than you can bind the sweet influence of the Pleiades. In the Acts of the Apostles we read that when Peter was healing the sick, those who were unable to get near to him because of the press of the crowd were laid by their friends along the street, so that when Peter passed by his shadow might fall on them and heal them. Figuratively speaking, this is always true in life. There is a shadow, an influence which falls from us noiselessly, but as inevitably and as irrevocably as the shadow of a tree.

This learned I from the shadow of the tree
Which to and fro did play upon the garden wall:
Our shadow selves, our influence may fall
Where we ourselves may never be.

Remember, you are a soul. Think of the man behind you, in front of you, and alongside of you in life. Search your heart, follow your trail of yesterday, last week, last year. Where would it have led anyone astray? Where would it have weakened another's faith? Where would it have kept a man from coming to Christ? If there is anything in your life, in your soul today that might hurt or blight another's soul, put it away from you, and by repentance and prayer come yourself into the fellowship of Jesus Christ. When you are in his fellowship, the influence which flows out from your life will always be for another's good.

**3**

# Soft Shoulders

*"Lot pitched his tent towards Sodom."*
— Genesis 13:12

Soft shoulders! This is a sign which is seen at the commencement of a stretch of new road, where the earth next to the concrete is freshly laid, and is not yet hard and compact. If the wheels of the car get off the concrete onto the loose earth, the soil is likely to give way and the car be overturned and ditched.

Along the highway of life there is what we might call a twilight region between light and darkness, a border territory between right and wrong. It is a strip of earth that lies just off the concrete of right and close to the ditch of transgression and disaster. All who get into the ditch of sin first cross the soft shoulders of questionable conduct. There is a way which leads to sin, upon which it is always dangerous to venture. There are acts which may not be described as positively sinful, but which certainly tend in that direction. There is a way which, although not yet involved in darkness, lies in the twilight between day and night. If the truth were told of the moral state of many persons, it could be expressed in this suggestive metaphor, "Soft Shoulders."

They are not yet clear off the highway or right, but far over to the edge, in the soft soil of questionable conduct, and unless there is a quick and decisive change of direction, moral disaster awaits them.

## I. SOFT SHOULDERS AT CHURCH

There are soft shoulders along the church highway. There are those who are on the way to the ditch of secularism, indifference, or alienation and bitterness. Once they started on this road with enthusiasm and earnestness, and with great promise of reaching their destination. But they had not long been on the way before their enthusiasm began to droop a little. Once the regular services of God's house were to them an engagement with the Lord from which nothing could keep them away. But after a time their attendance was not quite so regular. The Sunday evening or Sunday morning service was given up; Prayer Meeting and the Sunday School Class saw them no more; their own devotions, prayer, and the reading of the Bible, were intermittent.

The natural history of all such cases is either a complete sinking back into the world, or a barren, formal church relationship which makes such a name on the church roll a liability, rather than an asset to the church. To all who know themselves in this condition, who are on the "soft shoulders" in their religious life, I would speak the words of the angel to the Church at Ephesus: "Remember, therefore, from whence thou art fallen, and repent and do the first works; or else I will come to thee quickly, and will remove thy candlestick out of his place, except thou repent."

## II. SOFT SHOULDERS IN BUSINESS

There is such a thing as out-and-out dishonesty and falsehood; and there is also a kind of action and conduct, which, although it falls short of open fraud and wrong, leads in that direction and almost always ends there. By the road of evasion, insincerity, trickery, and equivocation, men come to grief. They may go on with their business, for they have stopped short of deeds which would bring the law upon them; but, in the minds of men, they are discredited, and are referred to as shifty, shady, tricky, and crooked. "A false balance is abomination to the Lord; but a just weight is his delight. The integrity of the upright shall guide them; but the perverseness of transgressors shall destroy them."

### III. SOFT SHOULDERS IN THE HOME

There are multitudes of homes in which personal relationships may be described with this metaphor, "soft shoulders." The open sore in American life, its crimson and crying shame, is its broken homes, its divorce-sundered families; and side by side with that its natural accompaniment, the open sewer of free love, companionate marriage, and kindred enemies of human happiness.

Sometimes these homes are broken and wrecked because of an inherent lack of character and Christianity on the part of the persons who have been joined together; and sometimes the wrecked home is due to neglect, or studied indifference, and the failure to give those small, but important, tokens of esteem and affection which are all the more necessary when people are living together day by day. It is possible for persons in the same home to permit themselves to drift so far apart that all desire to unite again has vanished. Again, by acts of disloyalty, or semi-disloyalty, and by permitting the affections to stray elsewhere, the union of the home is broken. Here they are standing on the dangerous and treacherous ground which may be called "soft shoulders," and just beyond lies the dismal ditch of separation and divorce.

## IV. SOFT SHOULDERS IN FRIENDSHIP
## AND PERSONAL RELATIONSHIPS

Few persons, men and women, get into the miry ditch of disaster and unhappiness and sleepless remorse by a single, sudden leap or plunge, or by a quick swerving of the wheel of life's car from the highway. Although imperceptibly, they have been for some time turning in that direction. What has happened looks like a sudden disaster or breakdown; but, in reality, it is the end of a long process of inner deterioration of heart and character.

When he chose the plains near Sodom and pitched his tent towards Sodom, Lot had no thought of becoming a citizen of Sodom. Yet he gradually drifted into that society, until his own daughters had married Sodomites, and only an angel's intervention saved him from destruction. Had anyone said to him, "Lot, within a year, Sodom will be your dwelling place and your home, and you will be the father-in-law of Sodomites," Lot would have been shocked. Yet so it came to pass; and the reason was that he "pitched his tent towards Sodom."

There are not a few who mean no harm in the liberties they give or take. They yield to the pleasure of this indulgence, and then another and another, till they are almost, or altogether, off the highway of right; mired in some dismal ditch, caught in some personal tangle from which they can hardly be extricated, and must drink a bitter cup of humiliation, sorrow and remorse.

Recently I received a letter from one who is interested

in the welfare of another soul. She asked prayers in behalf of a young woman who hitherto had stood for all that was good and has lived an honorable and Christian life, but who now is standing in the soft shoulders territory of a dangerous and a dishonorable friendship, the further indulgence of which can mean nothing but disaster and bitterness. There are many others besides this young woman who are in similar situations, and who might well be prayed for by all those who care for human souls. They are standing in the treacherous soft-shoulder soil of easy indulgence, and just beyond them, though covered perhaps with the green grass and the bright flowers of pleasure, is the deep and miry ditch.

## V. CONCLUSION

This is the grand chance of the preacher. The preacher draws the bow at a venture. If the arrow comes close, you are the one who knows that best of all. What an acquaintance, or even a close friend, or relative would like to say, but hesitates to say, and which, if said, might arouse resentment and do more harm than good, the preacher, drawing his bow at a venture, can say without offense or embarrassment.

Soft Shoulders! Avoid that treacherous territory which lies close to the ditch of sin. Keep to the center of the concrete of right. "Avoid the very appearance of evil." If you know that you have been travelling with one wheel on the soft shoulders of half-way transgression, and yet, in God's mercy, have not actually sinned, have by His goodness been kept out of the ditch, in spite of your own carelessness and folly, then thank God for it, and turn at once, immediately, to the hard and safe territory of right.

4

# Slippery When Wet

*"Their way shall be unto them, as slippery ways in the darkness."* — Jeremiah 23:12

"Slippery when wet!" That is the sign you see at the top of hills, on bridges, and on certain kinds of roads. You are warned that when the road is wet with rain or snow, it is slippery and your car is likely to skid. The road of life is slippery when he who travels it is wet. Drinking makes all roads slippery, and at all seasons of the year, and for all kinds of people — business men and professional men; youth, middle age, and old men.

## I. THE DISAPPEARANCE OF TEMPERANCE INSTRUCTION AND WARNING

When some of you were boys there was no lack of warning that the path of life was slippery when wet with drink. There were the Temperance Bands and the Tenth Legions. The pledge was presented in the home and at the Sunday School. I can well remember the day, and the room, in our home when one of my brothers and I were called in to sign a pledge. We saw nothing of drunken people and had little or no contact with victims of drink. But the fact that we were asked to sign a pledge that we would never drink intoxicating liquor, sank into our mind the truth that drinking is a dangerous thing.

I was examining some time ago an old Family Bible which belonged to one of the families of our church. In the space between the Old Testament and the New Testament there were the pages devoted to births, marriages, and deaths. And then a page that had a blank form for the signing of the Temperance Pledge. That goes to show how closely religion and the church in that day were linked with temperance principles and temperance instruction. The Bible was the symbol of that which was sacred and holy. It was a book devoted to the welfare of the soul. Therefore, it was most fitting that on one of those pages between the Old Testament and the New Testament there should be a page where the children could sign a pledge not to drink intoxicating liquor. If all children were so trained, and had such a pledge presented to them in their youth, the ravages of strong drink would be far less terrible and disastrous than they are.

Now and then someone quotes to me the saying of St. Paul when he counseled Timothy, who evidently was a frail, invalid sort of young man, to take a little wine for his stomach's sake. And, of course, for all liquor dealers and manufacturers the one part of the Bible at least, that they know well, is that chapter in St. John's Gospel where Jesus turned water into wine. However, it is well to remember that where one passage might be cited in favor of strong drink, there are many more passages which can be cited against it. From the Book of Genesis to the Book of Revelation the Bible rings with warnings against the curse of strong drink. It was when he became drunk that Noah lay uncovered and disgraced before his sons. It was when he was drunk that Lot committed incest with his daughters. It was when

he and his captains drank themselves drunk in their pa-
vilion that the king of Syria, Benhadad, and his army, were
beaten in battle. It was when Belshazzar was drunk that
the hand came out and wrote against the wall, "Thou art
weighed in the balances and art found wanting," and his
kingdom was given unto the Medes and the Persians. It was
when Nabal was drunk that he insulted David and shortly
afterwards died of a stroke. It was when Amnon was drunk
at the feast that Absalom slew him for his shameful crime
against their sister Tamar, a crime, no doubt, committed,
as most of such crimes are, under the influences of liquor. It
was when Ahasuerus was drunk that he made his infamous
proposal that the Queen Vashti should come in and expose
her beauty to the drunken revelers. What a trail of folly,
incest, adultery, and murder drunkenness leaves behind it
in the Bible! The Old Testament sums up its teaching on
the subject by saying, "Wine is a mocker, strong drink is
raging, and whosoever is deceived thereby is not wise." And
the New Testament sums up its teaching on the subject
by the warning of St. Paul, "No drunkard shall inherit the
Kingdom of God."

## II. THE PRESENT DAY INVITATIONS AND
## ENCOURAGEMENT TO DRINK

In contrast with the old warnings against drinking, today
everywhere men are invited to drink. There is the invitation
of custom. By that I mean the fact that liquor is sold and
drunk, not only in a few saloons, as in the old days, but
everywhere. I can remember groups of young men who
wanted to drink going behind the barn or an outhouse and
passing the bottle around. There was the recognition and
the consciousness on their part that it was something that

ought not to be done. The saloons, with their illuminated sign at the side, "Ladies' Entrance," were places against which youth could be warned. But now youth is accustomed to seeing people drink. Television resounds with the praise of liquor. Costly advertisements in the magazines tell of the excellence of various brands of whiskey. The great signs along the highways show men and girls drinking. It is only natural that with such a propaganda drinking should increase. Now, without any sense of shame, the long queues of men and women stand in line before the doors of the State Liquor stores. Satan always wins a point when he disguises himself as "an angel of light," and liquor has won a great victory by putting on the garment of respectibility, and disguising itself as the friend of man. A visitor from another planet would surely conclude that to drink is desirable and delightful, and one of the chief ends of man.

### III. DRINK IS STILL MAN'S GREATEST ENEMY

But whatever the advertisements and the voices over the radio say, and the pictures in the magazines, strong drink is still man's great enemy. Whatever path he takes, drink makes it slippery. The folly of our society today, and of our local and federal governments, is to think that by taxing liquor we diminish the injury which it does to society. A jackass one day, uncomfortable in the summer heat, went down into a stream to cool himself. As he was standing in the water, a leech fastened itself to his back and began to suck his blood. When the jackass demanded of the leech that he withdraw his presence, the leech proposed a compromise. For every ten drops of blood that he drew from the back of the jackass he promised to pay him back one drop as revenue. The jackass, thinking that he would gain by the proposition, gladly accepted it, But an owl, overhearing the conversation, remarked, "Only a jackass would fall for that kind of economics."

In one of the recent years the cost of births in the United States was $225,000,000.00; of marriages, $300,000,-000.00; of funerals, $25,000,000.00; but of drink, $1,427,-000,000.00! In other words, drink costs one and a half times as much as all the births, marriages and funerals together. The drinking man is the last to be hired and the first to be fired. I had a striking illustration of the financial folly of drink brought home to me recently. In North Carolina I took a taxicab from the station at Black Mountain to the Assembly Inn at Montreat. When I got out of the cab at the hotel, I asked the driver how much it was. He said, "Fifty." I handed him a dollar bill, and as he was making the change, he told me that the night before, Christmas Eve, he picked up a fare at the station, and drove the man, who had considerable "Christmas Cheer" in him, just a few blocks to the house where he desired to go. When they reached the house he said to the driver, "How much is it?" The driver answered, "Fifty." Whereupon, the man drew out his wallet and laid down fifty dollar bills on the seat of the cab, then asked, "Is that all right?" Which goes to prove that "a fool and his money are soon parted"; especially when the fool is made more foolish by liquor.

Alcohol plays its part, and a chief part, in accidents. Experiments made with chronic drinkers and nondrinking workers showed 44 accidents per hundred among the nondrinkers, but 123 accidents per hundred among the drinkers. In one locality 60 per cent of the accidents on the highway and 75 per cent of those injured and killed were cases where alcohol was the contributory cause.

But the chief count against drinking is the injury it does to man's moral and spiritual nature. It weakens self-control and makes man subject to his passions, instead of his reason and judgment. How often men arraigned for a crime make the plea, "I had been drinking, and did not know what I was doing." Xenophon, the Greek historian, relates this incident about Cyrus who attacked and conquered Babylon when Belshazzar and his nobles were drunk. Cyrus as a youth had been taught to shun the intoxicating cup. Once on a visit to his royal grandfather in Media, Cyrus asked to be permitted to act in the place of the cup bearer who served the wine to the King. Cyrus did everything to perfection, and was loudly applauded by the nobles present, who were delighted with his perfect imitation of the cup bearer, stepping grandly and solemnly about. The king, his grandfather, too, praised him, but called his attention to one omission — he had neglected to taste the wine, as the cupbearer always did before he handed it to the king. Cyrus answered that the reason he had not tasted the wine was that he thought it had been poisoned. Asked why he thought that, Cyrus said: "It was poisoned the other day when you made a feast for your friends on your birthday. I knew by the effects. The things you do not allow us boys to do, you did yourself, for you were rude and noisy. You could not even stand erect and steady. So I thought the wine which produced these effects must have been poisoned." There is a sermon on drinking which is unanswerable in its simplicity and in its power.

"Who hath woe? Who hath sorrow? Who hath redness of eyes? Who hath wounds without cause? They that tarry long at the wine; they that go to seek mixed wine." Because liquor makes the path of life slippery and dangerous, the wise course is that of total abstinence. Every drunkard was a moderate drinker. Even if a man thinks he can drink moderately without any injury to himself, still he must think of the effect of his example upon others. What if your drinking encouraged someone else to drink, and that man's drinking led to his downfall and ruin? Why drink wine, anyway, when you have good water to drink? On the fountain at Stratford upon Avon, where Shakespeare was born, the fountain given by the American philanthropist William Childs, is the inscription from Shakespeare's *Timon of Athens:*

> Here's that which is too weak to be a sinner,
> Honest water which ne'er left man in the mire.

John B. Gough, the great temperance orator, who used to thrill the multitudes with the story of his own battle with strong drink, and who once spoke in this church, used to recite with great effect the "Apostrophe to Water" in Judge Arrington's once popular book, *Paul Denton,* the story of a Methodist circuit rider in the southwest country. There is a possibility that in Paul Denton, Judge Arrington had in mind the famous circuit rider of Illinois, Peter Cartwright. It had been announced that the preacher would preach at a famous spring where there was plenty of good liquor for all who would attend. In the midst of the sermon a desperado arose and demanded, "Where is the liquor you promised?" "There," answered the preacher in tones of thunder, pointing at a spring gushing up from the bosom of the earth. "There is the liquor which God the Eternal brews for all his children.... And everywhere it is a thing of life and beauty; gleaming in the dewdrop, singing in the summer rain, shining in the ice gem until the trees all seem to turn to living jewels.... And weaving the many colored bow whose warp is the raindrops of heaven; whose woof is the sunbeams of heaven, all checkered over with the mystic hand of refraction.

"Still it is beautiful, that blessed life water! No poisonous bubbles are on its brink; its foam brings not murder or madness; no blood stains its liquid glass; pale widows and starving orphans weep not burning tears into its burning depths, no drunkard's shrieking ghost from the grave curses it in the world of eternal despair. Beautiful, pure, blessed and glorious. Speak out, my friends, would you exchange it for the demon's drink, alcohol?"

The road of life is always slippery when wet. How about the highway of your habits? What are your chances on the slippery road?

**5**

# Crossroads

*"At the parting of the way."* — Ezekiel 21:21

Crossroads! When we come to this sign on the highway, we slow down because of the risk of a collision with a machine crossing the road which we are following. But the sign is also an invitation to be sure about the route we want to take, and it also tells us that at this particular point we must decide which way we are going. To the left, or to the right, or straight ahead? One road will take us to one place; another road to a different place. If we are careless and indifferent at the crossroads, we are likely to get off our true course and travel anywhere but towards the place for which we have set out. If it's just a joy ride, or a journey of pleasure, it doesn't make much difference whether we get off the road or not. But since the journey along life's highway is not a joy ride, but a serious undertaking, to take the wrong road involves serious consequences. In the night, particularly, it is easy to make the wrong turning at the parting of the ways and be miles off the true course before we know it. Therefore, it is wise to slow up at the crossroads and scrutinize carefully, the directions which are posted there.

Along life's highway, we come frequently to places which may be likened to the crossroads or the parting of the ways. In Ezekiel's vision, the king of Babylon stood at the parting of the ways outside of Jerusalem. Roads are as old as humanity, and on all roads we come to the parting of the ways. At these turnings and partings we must decide in which direction we shall go. Sometimes these turnings on life's highway are not as clearly marked as the crossroads on the great highways of the country, and it may not be until long afterwards that we discover that we chose one route rather than another. Sometimes again, the turning point with adequate directions is clearly marked, and our conscience and our will plays its part. But whether we were fully aware of it or not, at these partings of the ways we made a choice which affected our destiny. In the crises of life's battle, the great issue may be consecrated into a few minutes of time. No one can escape personal religion. Everyone must decide and choose for himself; no matter what advice, or counsel, good or bad, may be given, we choose by ourselves and for ourselves.

> Thou hast a choice
> To choose is to create
> Remember whose the sacred lips that tell,
> Angels approve thee
> When thy choice is well.

## I. WE COME TO THE PARTING OF THE WAYS WHICH DECIDES OUR PLACE AND WORK IN LIFE

The massive gates of circumstances turn upon the smallest hinge of what, at the time, may seem to be trivial incidents. Perhaps you can trace your life as it is at present back to what, at the time, did not seem to be an important matter or decision, but which has proved to be the turning point of your life. One day you were not sure as to whether you ought to accept this position or take another, go to this school or go to another, take this course of study or some other. You asked someone's advice, and what he said opened up the door of the path that you have followed ever since. You decided to stop off at a town over night, and that town has been your place of work and your home ever since. You happened to go into a church and heard a sermon that started you to thinking along certain lines and that line of thought has had a dominating influence upon your life. You picked up a book one day, and what you read there turned you in the direction you have followed ever since. You went into a room and chanced to see a face — the face of your husband, your wife, your children. You gave on one occasion a negative, instead of an affirmative answer, or you said "yes," instead of "no"; and that "no" or that "yes" turned the river of your life into the channel where it now flows.

At first, this seems rather startling, that so much of one's life should depend upon what in the distance looks like chance. But when we lift this fact into the realm of faith, it has an assuring and calming effect, rather than otherwise, for it permits us to believe that Providence has a plan, that God has been guiding us when we knew it not, that our times are in His hand, and that there is a "divinity" which shapes our ends, rough hew them how we will.

## II. THERE IS A PARTING OF THE WAY, IN OUR MORAL AND RELIGIOUS LIFE

Take any man just as he is today — weak, miserable, degraded, the victim of evil habits; or strong, honorable, upright. Somewhere in his past, known or unknown at the time to the man, there was a parting of the way, a turning point of his life, a conviction, an alarm, an invitation, heeded or unheeded, a temptation to which he said, "No," or, "Yes." And what he did, or did not, what he chose and willed, at that time, has determined the nature of his life.

Some years ago, it was a source of no little satisfaction to me to get a letter from a member of the Tuesday Noon Club which let me know that some of the words which I speak are seed which falls upon good ground. This man told me that in common with several others in his company he was getting credit on the timesheet for working certain hours every other week, when actually his manager was giving them this time off. The office requires that full hours be shown on the time sheet. At the Tuesday Noon meeting, when I was speaking on the importance of decision, this man came to the decision that the only honest thing for him to do was to go to work on the time for which he got credit. He wrote me, thanking me that he got the impulse and the impetus at the Tuesday Noon Club. I am sure he has never regretted the decision he made. He was at the crossroads between honesty and dishonesty.

Sometimes these moral choices are made, and we hardly know that we are making them, just as one can turn off the right road on the highway and not know it till long afterwards. There we seem to choose almost automatically. Nevertheless, it is our choice, it is the registration of our will. It is the result of former choices and the momentum of acquired habits. Hence, the solemn importance of doing and choosing the right, as far as we see it, at all times, because this present choice is going to affect our decision in the choices in the future.

At other times the difference in the direction and the

turning of the way is clearly marked, and our choice of our way is made in full consciousness of what we are doing and where we are going. According to the old legend, the achievements of Hercules were determined by a choice which he made in his early manhood. He was confronted one day by two beautiful women — one was Duty, who invited him to take her path; the other, was Pleasure, and with her siren accents she invited Hercules to go her way. The legend embodies a parable of life; that is, that all men are confronted by a choice, and that as they choose, so they are.

A single choice at the parting of the way where temptation stands, like the King of Babylon outside the walls of Jerusalem, may forever fix the life course of a man.

One of the most distinguished and useful men in the religious world today has written that he regards a certain night in New York as a parting of the way and a turning point in his life. With his college friends he had gone down from Princeton to New York. Some of these men asked him to accompany them to a place where soul and body would have been defiled. He had the courage and independence to say, "no," and that refusal he looks back to now as a turning point in his life.

One can almost hear the clock of one's heart beat when one stops to remember that there are thousands of young men and young women confronted by a similar choice tonight; and if it were possible to do so, one would choose for them, so that their recollection of the parting of the way shall be as happy as that of the man to whom I have just referred. Alas for those with whom it will be otherwise. Yet every man must choose for himself. The choice he makes now, tonight, may determine the future course of his life and the destiny of his soul.

So from the heights of Will
Life's parting stream descends,
And, as a moment turns its slender rill,
Each widening torrent bends, —

From the same cradle's side,
From the same mother's knee, —
One to long darkness and the frozen tide,
One to the peaceful Sea!

### III. THE PARTING OF THE WAY WHERE THE SOUL DECIDES FOR OR AGAINST CHRIST

Today may be for someone such a parting of the ways. It is never safe to choose the wrong course now, because that may be the final course. It is never safe to postpone the right decision now, for that postponement may prove to be the final choice.

Today a man may turn to the right or the left, and from henceforth he is further and further away from eternal life. His earthly life goes on just the same as ever. He may be here in the church just as regularly as before. But whether he knows it or not, never again will he be as close to Christ and to Eternal Life as he is right now.

There is a time we know not when,
A place we know not where,
That marks the destiny of men,
For glory or despair.

There is a line by us unseen,
Which crosses every path,
The hidden boundary between
God's patience and His wrath.

Which way? Oh, if it be true that guardian angels wait and watch upon the individual soul, how earnestly now must they be waiting and watching! Without your wishing it or planning it, the great battle of destiny, with its issue of life and death, has swung in your direction, and you must take your part in it! It is only a step over the line; nevertheless the line is there, and you alone can take that step.

> Over the line, hear the sweet refrain,
> Angels are chanting the heavenly strain,
> Over the line. Why should I remain,
> With a step between me and Jesus?

**6**

# Stop — Look — Listen

*"Watch and pray."* — Luke 22:46

Stop! Look! Listen! This is the one highway sign which was well known even before the days of the automobile. On a post at the railroad crossing, the two transverse X-shaped planks, painted white, carried in large black letters the warning, "Stop! Look! Listen!" The same kind of sign is still to be seen, and sometimes with the grim embellishment of a skull and cross bones, the symbol of lurking death, or the picture of a car which had tried to beat the locomotive being hurled to destruction by the onrushing engine.

When the great Alexandrian grain ship on which St. Paul was being conducted a prisoner to Rome was driving before the storm through the Mediterranean, on the fourteenth night, Luke tells us, "The shipmen deemed that they drew near to some country." How did they know that they were drawing near to the dangerous cliffs of the isle of Malta? The only way they could have known it was by the sound of the breakers, the deep thunder of the waves breaking on the rockbound coast. Warned by that sound, the seamen at once lowered four anchors out of the stern. The warning which was brought to them by the thunder of the breakers was not in vain.

Warnings come to those who are slipping or drifting morally. Not by a single plunge or leap do men go down, but gradually, slowly, step by step. It is with them as when a rope suddenly breaks, but not until strand after strand has parted; or, as when a dam goes out, but not until the wall of the dam has been slowly undermined by the working of the water. So, before men's characters collapse and go down, and alas, how many thousands do, they have their warnings and pass over obstacle after obstacle raised up against them.

## I. CONSCIENCE IS A WARNING

How many times conscience has said to you and me, bound on some eager journey of desire, "Stop! Look! Listen!" There is a certain uneasiness, a feeling that all is not right within. Conscience hurts when we have done wrong; but it also pricks and warns before we do wrong. There is a certain native dread and shrinking from evil, and the penetration of temptation's lance produces, in hearts not yet hardened by sin, discomfort and pain; and the office of pain is always to warn.

When Elisha was prophet in Israel, and Benhadad, the king of Syria, was invading the lands and seeking to capture the king of Israel, the king of Syria was time and time again foiled in his plans by the warning which the man of God sent to the king of Israel. "And the king of Israel sent to the place which the man of God told him and warned him of and saved himself there, not once or twice." When the baffled and enraged king of Syria demanded to know who of his army was a traitor and gave away in advance its movements, one of his servants answered, "None, my lord, O

King; but Elisha the prophet that is in Israel telleth the king of Israel the words that thou speaketh in thy bed chamber." In the history of every man's struggle for righteousness, and in his battle with temptation, there is something comparable to this. There is, as it were, a "man of God" within our hearts who warns us in advance; and if we heed that warning of conscience we are safe.

> Then keep thy conscience sensitive,
> No inward token miss,
> And go where duty bids thee,
> Thy safety lies in this.

## II. THE EXPERIENCE OF OTHERS WARNS US

I saw sometime ago a statement by someone associated with the stage, that even if the pulpit should cease to declare the fact of sin, that virtue has its own reward, and that vice will be punished, the stage will continue to teach and to preach these doctrines. Whatever the effect of such teaching behind the footlights, always on the stage of life there is a solemn and impressive teaching of the ancient truth, and modern, too, that God is not mocked; that whatsoever a man soweth that also shall he reap; and that the way of the transgressor is hard.

In an interview once with a man just out of the Maryland penitentiary, I was struck with the fact of how strange a thing it is that men who get into evil ways pay no attention to the warnings which they receive. This man had Christian training and splendid background. But he was persuaded to become the accomplice of a fellow clerk who was playing the races, and together they robbed the bank. As always happens, after a brief period the robbery was detected, and he was arrested and sentenced to the penitentiary. When he told me his story I said to him: "You are an intelligent man. You must have read the newspapers and must have known what happened to other men who did what you were going to do. How could you think that you could prove an exception to the rule of exposure and punishment? Why did experience teach you nothing?" He answered, "Well, I see that now. But, like so many others, I didn't think of it at the time."

It was a saying of Terence, "This is a wise maxim, to take warning from others of what may be to your own advantage." Who, driving along the road and seeing a car overturned by the roadside or being towed away all smashed and broken by a wrecking car, has not said to himself, "There is a warning for me. I must be careful."

Always these danger signals are flashing in the lives of other men, letting us know when we draw near to some dangerous shore, inviting us to "Stop, Look, and Listen." What flaming lessons! What stern and earnest teachers! Everywhere we see men and women getting ensnared, entangled, soiled, defiled, broken, wrecked. How can we hear of this, read of it, see it depicted on the printed page, or elsewhere, without being warned thereby? If you have started just recently, or perhaps, who knows, have travelled far along the same path, be warned by what you see in the experience of others. O life, what a teacher thou art; how generous with thy lessons; how patient with thy unwilling scholars; how plain and unmistakable thy instruction; line upon line and precept upon precept! How eloquent thy pleadings! How sad thy farewell to the soul that would not be warned: "Turn you at my reproof; because I have called and ye refused, I have stretched out my hand, and no man regarded; but ye have set at naught all my counsel and would none of my reproof. I also will laugh at your calamity. I will mock when your fear cometh. Then shall they call upon me, and I will not answer. They shall seek me early, but they shall not find me, for that they hated knowledge and did not choose the fear of the Lord. They would none of my counsel; they despised all my reproof."

### III. PERSONAL APPEALS WARN US

Again, there is the warning which comes through private and personal entreaty or expostulation. Sometimes the most effective warnings come that way. Sometimes the most powerful sermons are preached to a congregation of one. Even the word of an evil person may serve to arrest and stop someone on the road to ruin. The rebuke of a low woman at an ale house brought John Bunyan to his senses.

The soul is the most valuable thing in the universe. When we think that someone's soul is in peril, we ought not to hesitate to say a word of entreaty or warning. In the words of the prophet, "Run, speak to that young man!" Or, "Run, speak to that young woman." Your word may be the saving word. "He that converteth the sinner from the error of his ways shall save a soul from death, and shall hide a multitude of sins."

### IV. OUR AFFLICTIONS AND TRIALS WARN US

Our religion teaches us that these things are for our good; that they are God's touch upon us to cleanse and purify our lives, and that however grievous and painful they may now seem, they yield the fruits of righteousness to those who profit by their warning. Therefore it is that the afflictions and trials which come to us, whether bodily, or in grief of spirit, in the course of nature, or wrought by the enmity and injury of others, serve to make us search our hearts and see if there be any evil way in us, if there has been the slightest departure from the way of right, or any sinking into the way of sin. "By these things," said the Hebrew king, after his dangerous illness, "men live."

Men are warned, too, by the Word of God, as it is preached in the church. This is the preacher's grand opportunity, to say something which he may soon forget, but which may ring forever in the mind of one of his hearers; and to do this very thing, to utter the word of warning, the minister is commissioned and ordained of God. God says to the minister what He said of old to Ezekiel: "Son of man, I have set thee a watchman unto the house of Israel. Therefore, hear the word of my mouth, and give them warning from me." If the watchman gave his warning and the wicked turned not, and perished in his iniquity, the watchman had delivered his own soul. But if he had not given the warning, and the wicked perished in his iniquity, his blood was required at the watchman's hands.

The preacher is set upon the wall to warn himself and others. At the end of his beautiful farewell to the elders of the Church at Ephesus, at the port of Miletus, Paul, after giving an account of his preaching, reminded them how he was pure from the blood of all men, for "by the space of three years, I ceased not to warn everyone night and day with tears." The closest friend or dearest relative may not speak the word of warning. The posters of warning displayed along life's highways may not be seen or read; or, if read, not regarded. But whoever fails, the prophet of God must be faithful to his task. He must not fail. He must declare the statutes of God, for by them are men warned.

Has anyone been slipping or drifting morally, getting

closer and closer to the dangerous reef of transgression? Has anyone been backsliding in his Christian life, declining in his spiritual life? Has anyone been postponing and putting off from day to day a decision for Christ? Has anyone been hardening his heart against the persistent whispers of the Holy Spirit? Then, let him be warned. Stop! Look! Listen! When those seamen on Paul's ship heard the thunder of the breakers and knew that they were drifting on a rocky shore, they at once let go four anchors out of the stern. Perhaps there is some man here today who ought to do that at once. Before the waves of judgment crash over you, take warning! Overboard with the anchors of repentance, determination, prayer, and faith! Then in the morning of salvation you will escape safe to the land.

# 7

# Beware of Falling Rocks

*"They shall be afraid of that which is high."*
— Ecclesiastes 12:5

Three years ago, at the close of the day, a bus loaded with workers returning homeward from one of the Pennsylvania steel mills was rolling rapidly along the road when suddenly a huge mass of earth and rock fell upon it and crushed out the life of twenty-five people. This was a disaster which no skill or caution on the part of the driver could have averted. It had nothing whatever to do with his management of the bus, or the condition of it, or the state of the road. It was what the insurance people and the seamen call, "An Act of God."

Frequently driving along the road you have seen that sign, "Beware of falling rocks." It is a sign which you will not see between central Ohio and Colorado, for in that vast stretch of territory the road passes no hills from which rocks might fall upon you. But in the hill country like that of Western Pennsylvania it is a frequent sign, and sometimes one will see on the road the fragments of rocks that have fallen from the cliffs above.

"Beware of falling rocks." But how can you beware of

that? Perhaps reading that sign you have asked yourself the question, "What is the course to pursue? How can I beware of those rocks which possibly may fall upon me? If I drive slowly, then the rock may come down on me before I get out of the way. If I drive rapidly, I might possibly get by before it falls. On the other hand, it might bring me up in disastrous collision with the rock that had just fallen in front of me." The fact is that there is little you can do to beware of falling rocks. You never know when they are going to fall.

I take that sign, then, "Beware of falling rocks," as a parable and type of those troubles and adversities which no caution can avoid and which have nothing to do with man's good conduct or bad conduct. These are the "acts of God," the appointment of his providence, and when they come, they come. The practical question is, How to face them when they come?

## I. THE FOLLY OF FEAR AND WORRY

Here is a driver going along a highway which skirts one of those cliffs where great rocks jut out over the road far above, and all the time he is wondering if one of those rocks will let go and come crashing down upon him. But what good will that worry do him? It will neither retain the rock nor will it loosen it. It has absolutely no effect upon the safety or the danger of the man's journey. That was what Jesus said, "Take no thought for the morrow," — that is, no anxious, troubled thought — "for the morrow will take thought of itself. Sufficient unto the day is the evil thereof. Which of you by taking thought can add one cubit to his stature?" And how true that is! By taking anxious thought about possible danger that may come down upon you, by worrying about losing your job, or your health, or your money, or your reputation, what defense do you build up? What burden was ever lightened, what blow ever averted, what poignant grief ever comforted, what cup of sorrow was ever pushed from the lips, what pain ever alleviated by taking anxious thought concerning it in advance?

We know how vain are the fears of our nightmares. Who is there here who has not had some lion or tiger, or wild bull, or serpent after him and just about to destroy him, and then awakened to find that there was nothing in it. So are many of our fears.

> Better never trouble trouble
> Till trouble troubles you;
> For you only make your trouble
> Double trouble when you do.

One day a peasant was driving his wagon into Constantinople when an old woman by the roadside asked him to give her a ride into the city where she was going to the market place. The peasant took her into his wagon and then after a little he looked at her in astonishment and fear and cried out "Who are you?" The old woman said, "I am the Plague." Thereupon the peasant ordered her to get down and walk. But she persuaded him to take her along upon the promise that she would not kill more than ten persons with the Plague. As a pledge of her promise she gave him a dagger, saying to him that that was the only weapon with which she could be killed. If she did not keep her promise, and killed more than ten persons with the Plague, then when he met her he could kill her with that dagger.

In Constantinople a hundred people died of the Plague. With the dagger in his hand, the angry peasant hunted high and low for the woman and at length finding her, he raised the dagger and was about to slay her. But the woman stopped him, saying, "I kept my promise. I killed only ten with the Plague. Fear killed the rest."

That legend is a true parable of life. Where other enemies of man kill their thousands, fear kills its tens of thousands. Fear is man's great enemy. The Bible is man's great friend, and therefore it is that the one thing which the Bible says to us more than all else is, "Fear not." From Genesis to the golden gates of the Apocalypse that is the word that echoes and re-echoes in the Bible — "Fear not."

## II. FAITH

Faith is the way to deal with the rocks that may fall upon us, and the rocks which from time to time do fall upon us. Faith delivers from fear. God, the apostle said, hath not given us the spirit of fear, but of faith and a sound mind. When the rocks do fall upon us, then faith is our victory, and our only victory. When the disciples thought they were going to perish that night in the storm on the sea of Galilee, and awakened Jesus, asleep on a cushion in the stern of the boat, and cried to him, "Master, carest thou not that we perish?" Jesus rebuked the winds and the waves, saying, "Peace, be still!" Then he turned to the disciples and said, "Why were ye afraid, O ye of little faith?" Profound insight there, to the secret of the strong Christian life! It is the lack of faith that makes us fear. Courage is born of faith. "Faith is the victory that overcometh the world."

There was once an English farmer who needed a hired man to help him with his work on the farm. He went to the Fair and walked around where the crowds were gathering in front of the tents and the booths, watching the Punch and Judy show, and the dancing bear, and all that goes on at a Fair. Then he remembered why he had come, to look for a hired hand. In the crowd he saw one strong, awkward, gawky young man, and stopping him he said, "What is your name?" The youth said, "My name is John." "What do you do?" "I work on a farm." "Do you know anything about farming?" "Yes, sir." "What do you know?" "I know how to sleep on a windy night." "You know what?" "I know how to sleep on a windy night." "That," said the farmer, "is no recommendation. I have plenty of men now who know how to do that well." And so saying, the farmer left him.

He interviewed many others, but found none who seemed to please him. He kept thinking about the first fellow he had talked to, and who had given him that strange answer, "I know how to sleep on a windy night." He did not feel like hiring a youth who said that was all he knew about farming; and yet there was an honest look in the man's eye. So he searched for him again and said to him, "You are a strange kind of farm helper, but come along, I will give you a chance."

The youth worked away for several weeks. One night a great wind came sweeping over the hills and moors and roared against the house and the barns and the outbuildings and the haystacks, and shrieked up and down the chimneys. The farmer heard it and leaped out of his bed. He knew by experience what that wind could do to his haystacks and his barns and cribs. Running into the attic where the hired boy slept, the farmer shook him by the shoulder and cried to him, "John, get up! The wind is taking everything!" The farmer shouted almost as loud as the wind itself, but John never heard it. He lay as still as a log.

Then the farmer left him and, hurrying downstairs, rushed out into the night to see what damage had been done. But all the stable doors were locked, the horses safe in the barn and the cattle in their stalls; the stacks of grain and hay were well roped and erect and all the fowl and the pigs and the sheep were safe. Then the farmer laughed to himself. Now he knew what the hired boy meant when he told him, "I know how to sleep on a windy night."

The wind will blow. You can count on that. If you haven't locked the doors and fastened the cattle and tied down the haystacks, it's too late to do it when the wind begins to blow. The time to do it is before the wind blows. That hired boy could sleep because he had done his work well.

The winds will blow. You can count on that. When the wind blows what will you do? As God said to Jeremiah, "How wilt thou do in the swelling of the Jordan?" Do you know the great Friend and Companion and Saviour, Jesus Christ?

The rocks will fall. We don't know when; but they are sure to fall; the rocks of grief and sorrow and temptation and sickness, and, at length, death itself. The sinners and the impenitent in the Book of Revelation called upon the rocks to fall on them and hide them from the face of him that sat upon the throne. That was the fear of a guilty conscience. But believers in Jesus, who have put their trust in him, know that no falling rocks can crush them or hide them from the love and the care of God.

8

# Detour

*"But the Spirit suffered them not."* — Acts 16:7

Detour! This highway sign is greeted with smothered groans, or ejaculations of impatience. The motorist glares at the sign and the barrier across the road as if he were half-determined to go on regardless of sign or barrier. But if so, he runs the risk of danger, and ultimately meets with failure and is compelled to turn back. The detour is rough, dusty, and at right angles to the direction in which he has been traveling. Yet, it is a necessary change of route, and, if followed patiently, brings the traveler back to the main highway.

Life has many detours. After many miles of smooth going in fine spirits and rapid progress, suddenly we come upon this sign, "Detour," and are arrested by the barrier. Then we leave a fine road for the rough road and life is heavy and labored and difficult. What are some of the things in life which we may liken to a Detour?

## I. SICKNESS

This man goes strongly and joyously along. Others might fall out of the ranks through weariness or sickness, but not he. Perhaps the goal has been almost reached, the prize almost attained, the book almost finished, business almost established; then sickness stops the procession, and everything must wait. Yet there may be hidden good in this arrest and detour. Perhaps a pride of mind, a self-sufficiency, was there which made God less and less. Sickness taught the man his weakness and his dependency on God.

One of the greatest of the kings of Israel was Uzziah, soldier, builder and administrator, who brought the Hebrew Kingdom to what was perhaps its highest pitch of glory and splendor. In the midst of this noonday splendor, the great king forgot God and was smitten with leprosy. The ancient Chronicler is not only the narrator of facts, but the prober of the heart, when he writes of Uzziah: "His name spread far abroad, for he was marvellously helped till he was strong. But when he was strong, his heart was lifted up to his destruction, for he transgressed against the Lord his God." There are perils in strength and success, and those who have been turned aside from this goal by sickness or some other providence have learned in this way their dependence upon God.

Again, sinful habits may have been slipping the chains of their bondage about a man, enslaving him beyond his own knowledge and consciousness. Then sickness threw him on his back, and in moments of meditation and self-examination he realized his moral condition; and in the heat of his meditation the chains of evil habits were melted.

At the time of his serious sickness and operation in August, 1893, Grover Cleveland wrote: "I have learned how weak the strongest man is under God's decrees; and I see in a new light the necessity of doing my allotted work in the full apprehension of the coming night." Thus to be laid aside for a season from our task, not only teaches us humility, but makes us more earnest and industrious when strength returns to us. This was the verdict of David after his trouble: "It was for my good that I have been afflicted." This was the verdict of Hezekiah after his near approach to the gates of death: "By these things men live."

## II. DETOURS OF SORROW AND GRIEF

Fair skies, soft winds, fine companionship, rapid progress. Then this formidable sign uprears itself — "Detour. Go by the way of the Valley of Humilitation, pass through Gethsemane, and turn to the right at Calvary." Thus, suddenly, the springs of life break, and all the "go" is taken out of existence. No design, no objective, no incentive. A bereaved friend wrote me some time ago, "My sister and I are very lonely. My son was the heart of our home. He was so dear to us; and all the love we gave to him he returned in full measure. We never realized what a wonderful road we were traveling until we came to the sign, 'Detour.' Now the road ahead seems difficult indeed. But we both know that God will give us grace for the day. God has been wonderful to us and so gracious to our son."

By his own mysterious detour God may be leading us to greater goals. The sickness and death of her child inspired Harriet Beecher Stowe to write Uncle Tom's Cabin. Milton lived to discover that he was to do more than just "stand and wait." But at the time he wrote the famous sonnet on his blindness, it seemed to him that his affliction was to stand as a barrier between him and his great dream of writing something "such as men would not willingly let die." So he said:

When I consider how my light is spent

Ere half my days in this dark world and wide,
And that one talent which is death to hide
Lodged with me useless, though my soul more bent
To serve therewith my Maker, and present
My true account, lest He, returning, chide;
"Doth God exact day-labour, light denied?"
I fondly ask. But Patience, to prevent
That murmur, soon replies: "God doth not need
Either men's work, or his own gifts. Who best
Bear his mild yoke, they serve him best.
    His state
Is kingly; thousands at his bidding speed.
And post o'er land and ocean without rest;
They also serve who only stand and wait."

### III. THE DETOUR OF BAFFLED DESIRES, PLANS, AND AFFECTIONS

Sometimes you hear a man say that life has turned out for him just about as he had planned it. But more often what we see is men contrasting what they had planned and purposed with what has actually taken place.

First of all, there are the high and honorable ambitions of life. There is Paul on his second Missionary Journey. With his ever burning zeal and immense energy, he is on his way first, to Ephesus, the great city in that part of the world. What a place, thought Paul, to preach the gospel! Under the very shadow of the Temple of Diana! There proclaim the glories of the Temple not made with hands! But the Holy Spirit forbade him to preach there. Then he turned northward to go into Bithynia, where, along the Black Sea, were great and populous cities. No doubt Paul was greatly discouraged and perplexed at these barriers which were flung up in front of him, and wondered at this detour which took him down through Mysia to Troas. But there he learned the reason; for it was there the man from Macedonia appeared and besought him to cross over to Europe and help them. Had he gone to Ephesus alone, or had he been permitted to go into the remote North along the Black Sea, Athens, Corinth and Rome might not have heard the accents of the gospel from his prognostic lips.

Thus God's detours lead us to greater goals than we ourselves had in mind. God sometimes disappoints us and baffles us in order to make us succeed. If Phillips Brooks had succeeded as a schoolmaster, he would never have stood in the pulpit, to move men with his mighty ministry. If Frederick Robertson had got his commission in the British Army, he would never have written the sermons which still throb with his great and yearning spirit. If Hawthorne had been retained at the Custom House, he never would have written those wonderful studies in the deep places of human sin, and sorrow and love.

Once more there are those desires and ambitions which have nothing to do with the glittering stage of publicity, but center about one's intimate, personal life, but none the less real and cherished because of that. The capacity for friendship and affection must exist in some degree in every breast. Yet nothing could be plainer than that sometimes those who have this capacity the most highly developed have the least opportunity for the expression of it. Could we but listen to the deep undertone of humanity's ocean, we could catch the music of these unfulfilled hopes, baffled endeavors, and broken desires. Thousands of hearts have been flung back upon themselves, and wondered why. Yet the Great Road Commissioner who plans our journey knows best.

On life's highway we must trust His signs, and have faith that in the very baffling of our desires God is bringing to us some great and good thing.

Moses was heavy and sore at heart when, in spite of his pleading, God forbade him to enter the Promised Land and buried him on Nebo's lonely mountain. But in the end Moses discovered that that grave on Nebo's lonely mountain was just a detour on the road of Mt. Tabor, when he and Elijah appeared in glory and talked with Jesus of His atonement, His decease, which He should accomplish at Jerusalem.

> O lonely tomb in Moab's land,
> O dark Beth Peor's hill;
> Speak to these anxious hearts of ours
> And teach them to be still.

Time's detours have an eternal purpose in them. At length, even though it be as far along as the gates of death, God brings us back to the King's Highway, the road on which there are no more detours, and which leads straight on to the Palace of the King.

**9**

# Men Working Ahead

*"Am I my brother's keeper?"* — Genesis 4:9

The hard-boiled Marine general of the First World War, and after, Smedley Butler, once related how on a trip through Italy in the early years of Mussolini's reign, he was driving one day in Mussolini's state car from Rome to Florence. Passing through one of the Italian towns with their narrow streets, the car struck a child and hurled it to the pavement. General Butler, in distress, said to Mussolini: "The car has struck a child." Mussolini, ordering the chauffeur to drive on, answered Butler: "What is a life of a child in the life of the state!"

That was Mussolini's way of looking upon the life of a helpless child. In the business of the state and in his plans for regimenting Italy, the life of a single child was not worthy of consideration. That was the point of view, too, of Cain, the first murderer. When God asked him, "Where is Abel, thy brother," Cain answered, "I know not. Am I my brother's keeper?" There are two kinds of people who travel the highway of life. Those who have only their own interests and welfare at heart, and those who think of others and feel their obligation toward their fellow travellers.

"Men working ahead!" That is a sign you frequently see put up in yellow letters on a steel frame in the middle of the road when you come to a section of the road where men are at work, either painting division lines for the traffic or repairing the surface of the road. The sign warns you to drive cautiously lest your car should strike and injure one of those who are at work.

## I. WE ARE STEWARDS OF MEN

Always along the highway of life there are other men travelling and other men at work. Always your fellow men are on the road, some of them working, some of them struggling, some tempted, some sorrowing, some despairing. Drive carefully lest you injure them. Every one of us exerts an influence for good or evil as we travel the path of life. We ought always to think of those men who are at work on the road. They have desires and ambitions just as you have. They have homes which they like to reach at the end of the day when the shadows are falling. They have loved ones who are waiting to greet them just as you have. When you think of that, then you will want to deal justly and kindly with every other man whom you meet and pass on Life's Long Highway.

At the very beginning of man's history we have the record of the judgment pronounced upon Adam after the Fall— "Cursed is the ground for thy sake." Here we have the first record of the influence and the trial of a soul. Here at the fountain head of history God says to man, "Cursed is the ground for thy sake." Something very solemn and arresting about that. Because of what you have been, or said, or did, this part of the earth is cursed or blessed. Every life has a collateral influence. Every step that we take makes a chord vibrate somewhere else. The wind blows the seed from the garden of man's life into the garden of another man's life. It may be the seed of fruit or flower, or it may be the seed of thorns and thistles. In the Old Testament we hear that monotonous refrain, "Jeroboam, the son of Nebat, who made Israel to sin." So there are lives who, as they traveled along life's highway, have hurt and poisoned and saddened and injured other lives. For their sake the ground over which they traveled was cursed to other men.

There is a legend that Alexander the Great once sent in to a certain province a beautiful maiden whose breath was like perfume of richest flowers. But all her life she had lived amid poison, inhaling it until her body was full of poison. Flowers presented to her withered on her breast, and if she breathed on a bird, it fell dead. The legend embodies the truth that there are those who so live that in their presence that which is pure and beautiful withers and dies under the blighting and corrupting poison that goes from them. Voltaire had for an instructor a French Abbe who, although in sacred orders, was an unbeliever, and instructed his charge in the principles of unbelief. He also introduced him to dissipated circles in Paris. It was not strange therefore that with that kind of example and instruction Voltaire became a polished and satirical enemy of the Christian faith. Alas, how many homes and hearts and gardens have been hurt and cursed through the evil influence of others! The Bible warns us against all kinds of temptation and Christ taught us to pray, that we might not be led into temptation. But the Bible also has much to say about the sin of tempting others. When men are summoned before the prophets of God and sentenced for their transgression, that note is always sounded. They are judged and condemned, not only for what they have done to themselves, but because of the effect of their transgression upon others.

In the introduction to his famous book, *Tom Brown's Schooldays,* Thomas Hughes describes the character of the great master of Rugby, Thomas Arnold, and tells how the great teacher took pains to remind the boys under him of the effect of their influence upon others: "He taught that in this wonderful world no boy or man can tell which of his actions are indifferent and which not, and how by a thoughtless word or look we may lead a brother astray."

There was a man who once had a dream that he was in hell. When asked to give an account of what he had seen and heard there — if there were flames there, and suffering, and wrecked and malignant creatures with whom he was compelled to associate, and if the place resounded with oaths of blasphemy — he said: "Yes, all that was there. But there was something far worse than that," he said, "I was compelled to face my influence. I knew that I had lived a godless life, and that I deserved punishment, for I had scorned and rejected Jesus Christ; but my sorest pain was to see the effect that my life had had upon others."

## II. WE CAN HELP OR HURT PEOPLE

It is as easy to help people working on the road as we drive along life's highway as it is to hurt them. One cold October night in 1842, a young man twenty-five years of age, now an unemployed actor and bookbinder, homeless, aimless, and all but hopeless, his body weakened with habitual indulgence in whiskey, his clothing thin and threadbare, was staggering along the street in Worcester, Massachusetts, when a stranger touched him on the shoulder and said to him, "You have been drinking today." The kindness of his voice dispelled any anger which the drunkard otherwise might have felt.

"Yes, sir," he replied, "I have."

"Why do you not sign the pledge?" the other man said to him.

The young man thought a moment and then said to the man that he had no hope of ever becoming a sober man; that he was without a friend in the world; that he fully expected to die very soon and did not care whether he died drunk or sober. The other man took him by the arm and asked him how he would like to be as he once was, respectable and esteemed, well clad, sitting in a place of worship, able to meet his friends. "Oh," the young man answered, "I should like all these things first rate, but such a change cannot be possible."

"Only sign our pledge," said the other, "and I will warrant that it shall be so."

Writing a quarter of a century afterwards, he said: "Oh, how pleasantly those words of kindness and promise fell on my crushed and bruised heart! I had long been a stranger to feelings now awakened in my bosom. A chord had been touched which vibrated to the tone of love. Hope once more dawned. On the instant I resolved to try."

He did try. That night he drank himself into insensibility, but the next night, clad in an old brown overcoat buttoned up to the chin to cover his ragged suit of clothes, he went to the Temperance meeting and signed with shaking, palsied hand, and in crooked characters, his name to the pledge.

Within a few months that young man was thrilling and charming multitudes. In his day and generation he addressed more thousands of his fellow men than any man of his age and day. For the despairing ex-actor and bookbinder, staggering hopelessly along the streets of Worcester that night, and whom the stranger touched on the shoulder, was none other than John B. Gough. All that Joel Stratton did was to touch him on the shoulder and speak a word of kindness.

When we travel the highway of life it is wise to think not only of those whom we pass on the way, and those who may be ahead of us, but also about those who are to follow us, and do what we can to help them. One of the greatest things about Joshua, that Great Heart of the Old Testament, was his noble thought and desire for the generation in Israel which was to follow him. The approaching sunset of his own life in no respect diminished his faith or his zeal for God. "Cleave unto the Lord your God," he said, "for the Lord your God, He it is that fighteth for you, as He hath promised you." To plan for the future, to think of those who come after us, whether it be the planting of a tree which shall give its shade to some weary one on the pilgrimage of life long after our own pilgrimage is over; or to plan that our money shall serve some worthy Christian purpose when we are gone, to live so that our memory shall be blessed to those who come after us, that is always a mark of high faith and noble courage.

> An old man going a lone highway,
>   Came at the evening cold and gray
>   To a chasm vast and deep and wide.
> The old man crossed in the twilight dim,
>   The sullen stream had no fear for him.
> But he paused when safe on the other side.
>   And built a bridge to stem the tide.
> "Old man," said fellow pilgrim near,

"You are wasting your strength building here,
Your Journey will end with the closing day,
    You never again shall pass this way.
You've crossed the chasm deep and wide,
    Why build you this bridge at eventide?"
The builder lifted his old gray head,
    "Good Friend, in the path I've come," he said,
"There followeth after me today
    A youth whose feet must pass this way.
This chasm that's been as naught to me
    To that fairhaired youth may a pitfall be;
He, too, must cross in the twilight dim.
    Good Friend, I'm building this bridge for him."

## III. WE CAN TRAVEL AS JESUS TRAVELLED

The greatest of all travellers along life's highway, the Divine Traveler Himself, is the one who tells us how to pass along the road. He did it in the beautiful parable of the Good Samaritan. A lawyer, testing Him, wanted to know what he should do to inherit eternal life. Jesus asked him, what the Law said on the subject. The lawyer quoted the summary of the commandments: "Thou shalt love the Lord thy God with all thy heart and with all thy soul and with all thy strength, and with all thy mind, and thy neighbor as thyself." Then Jesus said to him, "Thou hast answered right. This do, and thou shalt live." But the lawyer said to Jesus, "And who is my neighbor?" Jesus answered with the story of the man who went down to Jericho and fell among thieves, which stripped him of his raiment and wounded him and departed leaving him half dead. After a time one of the priests came along and saw the man lying there on the highway where the robbers had left him. But the priest probably said to himself: "If the man is dead, it would be defiling for me to touch him. If I did stop to help him, officers of the law might happen to come along and, seeing me working over the man, might conclude that it was I who robbed him. Furthermore, the robbers are probably not far away, and if I stop to care for this man, they will attack me, and leave me in as bad a state as they left him." And so he passed on the other side.

Then came a second traveler, a Levite. He, too, making no doubt the same excuses as the priest, passed by on the other side. And last of all came the Samaritan. When he saw the man lying there, weltering in his blood, he knew at once that he was a Jew, and that if he himself, a Samaritan, had been lying there and the Jew passing by, he would have done nothing for him, for the Jews had no dealings with the Samaritans. The Samaritan, too, was subject to the same inconvenience and danger in stopping to help the wounded man that the other two would have experienced. Yet it was the Samaritan, from whom the least might have been expected, who stopped and dressed the wounds of the poor man, set him on his ass, conducted him to an inn, and put him up there at his own expense.

Having told this great tale, Jesus now answered the lawyer's question, "Who is my neighbor," by asking another question: "Which now of these three, thinkest thou, was neighbor unto him that fell among the thieves?" And he said, "He that showeth mercy on him." Then said Jesus unto him, "Go, and do thou likewise."

That is the way to travel along Life's Highway. And when we travel that way it leads us at length to the King's **Country.**

# 10

# Dangerous Hill

*"Wilt not thou deliver my feet from falling?"*
— Psalm 56:13

Our theme today is suggested by another roadside sign — "Dangerous Hill — Use Lower Gear." It is a sign posted at the top of hills where the grade is steep, and the road winding. My observation has been that this is a road commandment more observed in the breach than in the keeping of it. Few seem to pay attention to it. When I ask why, they tell me that is a sign for beginners. Yet every now and then we hear of accidents which have happened on these hills, and not to beginners, but to experienced drivers. Had they observed the admonition of the sign, there would have been no wreck and disaster.

Reading so frequently this highway sign, "Dangerous Hill — Use Lower Gear," I fell to thinking of the place that such a sign might take in the warnings which are posted along the highway of life; and of those circumstances and conditions when there is a downward descent grade where precaution and care are necessary.

Wherever men meet with temptation, this sign may always be posted, "Dangerous Hill." The use of that tremendous three-lettered word, Sin, will spare the preacher an immense amount of rhetoric, for sin tells the real story of what has happened and the results of what has happened.

91

Just as drivers on the highway roll heedlessly by these signs, and disregard them as posted for someone else and not for themselves, so it is the custom of men to regard temptation as dangerous for someone else, but not for themselves.

## I. THE UNLIKELY TEMPTATION

Thousands of men are wrecked on the hill of what they considered improbable, if not impossible, temptations. When the thing has happened, men say, "Who would have thought it?" "The last person in the world I would have supposed . . .," etc., etc. In his Autobiography, Senator George F. Hoar speaks of the atrocious murder committed by one of the faculty at Harvard when he was a student there, and says, "John W. Webster gave lectures on chemistry and geology. There was no person among the faculty at Cambridge less likely to commit such a bloody and cruel crime as that for which he was executed." On the whole territory of temptation, whether we are going down a hill which we think is safe for us, although dangerous for others, or descending a hill which is admittedly full of peril, the wise thing is to take precaution, to watch and to pray.

One of the striking things about the personalities of the Bible is how they fell where they were supposed to be strong. Moses was a meek man; yet he fell under the temptation of arrogance and anger, when he smote the rock in the wilderness. David was one of the most spiritually-minded men of the Bible, yet he fell terribly before a temptation in the flesh. Peter was naturally a brave and courageous man; yet fear made him deny his Lord, and that in no unwarned territory, but on a hill posted with Christ's own words, "Satan hath desired to have you that he may sift thee as wheat."

We read recently of a strange disaster on the Pennsylvania Railroad. The "Sunshine Limited," bound for Texas and Mexico, had climbed the mountains west of Altoona and stopped on the top, beyond the tunnel, near Gallitzin, to dismiss the helper engine. In some way the last Pullman became detached from the rest of the train and began to move, at first slowly, down the grade toward Altoona, but all the time gathering momentum and speed, until it crashed into the side of the mountain on one of the great curves. All the efforts that were made by the brakeman, and the heroic porter, who died in the crash, were unavailing to stop the car in its runaway down the mountain. The farther it went the less effect the brakes had on it.

## II. GET READY IN ADVANCE

When a machine has attained high speed going down a hill, it is impossible to do anything to arrest its speed. That was something which ought to have been attended to at the start. It is so with the hill of temptation. Christ said to the disciples, "Watch and pray, that ye enter not into temptation." There is a sense in which men enter into temptation, and once in it are beyond all rescue. This evidently was what Christ was thinking. In their present peril He warns the disciples against drifting or slipping into a place where they will be sure to fail. When the baser elements of human nature are aroused, when passions come out of their dens seeking their prey, then you cannot argue or expostulate or plead with them. One might as well reason with a hurricane, or expostulate with an enraged tiger, or invoke pity from a cobra. Then resolutions, purposes, aspirations, considerations of honor, memories of innocence can no more bind and hold one than the green withes with which the

Philistines tied Samson. The only safe and wise plan is to take precaution in advance and keep these things under control. So the Apostle said that he "kept the body under." He went down hill in a lower gear. Meditation, prayer, occupation, and companionship will help to do this.

### III. DANGEROUS HILLS PLEASANT AT FIRST

There is no need to enumerate the different kinds of temptation, because we all know what these are; and just as the descent of a hill is at first easy and pleasant, but farther on full of danger and possible disaster, so there are temptations which in the beginning have pleasant associations, but the end thereof is death. The temptation to unbelief is one that ought not to be forgotten, for this is as definite, seductive, subtle, and alluring as any other, and, if yielded to, its blight for the soul is worse than any other. In the fellowship of those who mock at faith and the great principles of religion a man must be on his guard. The one who finds himself slipping out of religious habits, such as prayer and public worship, needs to beware lest suddenly he find himself in the sunless bog of infidelity. Even a formal church attendance is more of a moral anchor than we think.

### IV. A WARNING FOR US ALL

Watch and pray, lest ye enter into temptation. Certainly this sermon is above nobody's head, and underneath no one's experience and necessity. On the hill of danger the traveller will do well to heed the warning which the roadway commissioners have posted, and on the hill of life it will be wise for us to accept what the Bible has to say about life and its perils, and particularly what it has to say about our own hearts. A faithful study of our own hearts will do much to disentangle us from the snares of flattery, and, as Dean Swift has said, "will let him know more evil of himself than anyone else can tell him; and when anyone speaks ill of him, he rather thanks God that he can say no worse. For could his enemy but look into the dark and hidden recesses of his heart, he considers what a number of impure thoughts he might there see, brooding and hovering like a dark cloud upon the face of the soul."

There is a legend that Augustine shortly after his conversion, accosted on the street by a former mistress, turned and walked in the opposite direction. Surprised, the woman cried out, "Augustine, it is I!" But Augustine, proceeding on his way, cried back to her, "Yes, but it is not I!" What he meant was that there was a new Augustine and that this new Augustine would avoid the territory and very appearance of evil.

As physicians test the body for weakness or disease or pain, so we, too, can test the moral health of the soul. Are there things which once won our enthusiasm, but to which we are now cold? Are there things we can do without compunction of conscience which once would have cost us a sleepless night? These and other tests will let us know if we are on the down grade, and whether or not it is time for us to put on the emergency brake.

Unless dominated by a stronger influence, human life will be ruled by the baser desires and instincts. The lower instead of the higher will rule. This stronger, counteracting influence is found in Christ in the heart. There is a story about the temptation of St. Anthony, that when the tempters in fearful and divers forms were assailing him, and it seemed that he would be conquered, he suddenly saw the light of the face of Christ, and everything was changed. The tempters were stripped of their power, and the battle was won.

Always when one preaches a sermon like this, one will be thinking that there will be those for whom it is advice in the past tense, a sign set up before them after disaster has been encountered. What they must hear, then, is not how to avoid such a disaster, but how to be delivered out of the results of folly and sin. Here it is that the gospel sounds its grandest note. If Christ is a great Teacher and a great Warner, He is, thank God, a greater Saviour. Christ restores and redeems from the hurt and bondage of sin those who repent. But the repentance must be genuine, earnest and faithful. Where this is the case, let those who have been hurt or wounded by evil have no discouragement or despair of spirit. Christ forgives, cleanses, restores! "He restoreth my soul." "Though your sins be as scarlet, they shall be as wool! Though they be red like crimson, they shall be as white as snow."

11

# Road Ends

*"The end of that man is peace."* — Psalm 37:37
*"The end of the wicked shall be cut off."*
— Psalm 37:38

This is a sign which you sometimes see at the end of a street in the city, or as you drive along a road in the country — "Road Ends." It tells you that you can go that far and no farther, that beyond that there is no road.

So on the journey of life we come to a place where the road, so far as this world is concerned, comes to an end. When you come to the end of the road you have reached a destination. Hence, we ask ourselves the question, or ought to, "What lies beyond the end of life's journey? Is this all there is to it? Is there no beyond?"

Another sign that I remember seeing was this: "Think of tomorrow!" It was, no doubt, a sign warning the motorist and the traveller against the dangers and injuries which might follow reckless and careless driving. Let him think of his future welfare; that is, let him remember that tomorrow he will not want to lie in a hospital or in a morgue. But we lift this warning into its highest significance. Think of tomorrow! Think of the life after death. If man ended when the road ended; that is, the road of life; at fifty, or three

score and ten, or eighty, then it would make but little difference whether you thought about tomorrow or not, for
there would be no tomorrow. But if there is a tomorrow,
then it behooves us to think about it. Young in his *Night
Thoughts* said truly, "All men think all others mortal but
themselves." That is a common trait. The ultimate fact in
life we rarely apply to ourselves.

## I. THINK OF TOMORROW IN RELATIONSHIP
## TO THOSE ABOUT YOU IN THIS LIFE

The time comes when, so far as your relationship with
them is concerned, nothing can be changed. When the silver
cord is loosed and the golden bowl is broken, then, however
much we might have wished that we could change things, it
is now impossible. What we have written we have written.
The question, then, to ask yourself is this, "Is my relationship with my fellow man, with those near to me, with the
members of my own family, such as I am willing to contem-
plate as final, if life's road should come to an end tomorrow?" Remember what Thomas Carlyle had to say about the
wife whom, he realized, he had somewhat neglected in his
studies and in his writings: "Oh that I had you yet for five
minutes by my side, that I might tell you all!" And those
other words, too, which he wrote, "Cherish what is dearest
while you have it near you, and wait not till it is far away.
Blind and deaf that we are; Oh think, if thou yet love any-
body living, wait not till death sweep down the paltry little
dust clouds and dissonances of the moment, and all be at
last so mournfully clear and beautiful when it is too late."

There is a very old and a very impressive story of a youth
greatly beloved who died. In the next life he besought the
gods to let him return to this world for just one day, a day

44885

that was one of the least notable, one of the most ordinary days of his past life. The gods granted his request. He appeared again just as he had been at the age of fifteen in his old home. As he entered the living room his mother passed by him engaged upon some household task. Then he stepped out into the yard; and his father, busy with some work, and carrying tools in his hand, gave him an indifferent glance and passed on. Then the youth awoke to the fact that we are all dead; that we are only really alive when we are conscious of the treasure we have in our friends and loved ones. A piercing parable of truth. And since that is so, then how awake and alive we ought to be before the road comes to an end.

## II. WE OUGHT TO THINK OF TOMORROW IN CONNECTION WITH THE LIFE TO COME

This life is a trial for the life to come, and the final decisions and choices of this life cannot be revoked when the end comes. This is the life when we have opportunity for repentance. "Now is the accepted time and now is the day of salvation."

I remember a visit I paid once to the famous Strasburg Cathedral. In the south transept there is a famous clock. It not only preaches from hour to hour a great and solemn sermon, but it is a monument to the greatness of the human mind. Among its many intricate devices is one which marks the eclipses. So ingenious is the combination that it will last forever. As long as the earth wheels around the sun, that device, if it be preserved, will mark the eclipses.

At the hour of noon statues of the Twelve Apostles emerge and pass in reverent procession before the figure of Christ, who lifts his hand to bless them, while a cock flaps

Lincoln Christian College

his wings and crows three times. In the center are four figures representing the four ages of life, and in the midst of them stands Death. At the first quarter, glad childhood emerges and strikes the bell; at the second quarter, rosy Youth comes forth; at the third, sober Manhood comes forth and lifts his robust arm; and at the last quarter, feeble and decrepit Old Age lifts wearily his hammer to strike. When he is finished, Death lifts his arm and strikes the hour — Childhood, Youth, Manhood, Old Age, Death.

Some of those who stood watching the clock that day in the Cathedral belonged to life's first quarter; some to youth's golden morn; some to manhood's sober day, and some to the last quarter and the feebleness of old age; and one could see too plainly that ere long death would lift his hammer and strike the passing of their life.

To stand and watch the figures strike the quarter hour, one after the other, was subduing, impressive, solemnizing. It made one think of applying his heart unto wisdom. As he put himself in one of the four groups, one wondered how much time was left — the third stage, the fourth, or soon the stroke of death. It made one ask oneself, "What have I done with my life? What am I doing with it now?"

Even while the curious onlookers stand and silently watch the hands of that clock proceed around the face of the dial, and one after the other the five figures come forth to strike their blows, my life, your life, is marching inexorably onward to the end of the road. No prayer, no entreaty, no physicians' skill, no tears can then hold it back. The Road Ends.

### III. CONCLUSION

There are some things which can be done only in this life, before the road ends; and one of these things, and the greatest thing, is repentance. "It is appointed unto all men once to die, and after that the judgment." There is no reason to think that there will be any opportunity for repentance and faith in the life to come. It would take all the meaning out of the urgent pleadings of the Holy Spirit, as we hear his voice in the Scriptures, calling upon men to repent and to believe on Christ, if, regardless of whether they repented or not, they would have a chance to do so in the world to come.

On the stormy southwest coast of England, there is a church whose towers are silent. No bell ever rings for the living or tolls for the dead. There is a legend that a ship was once beating its way along that shore, and that it had on board the bells designed for this church of Bottreaux. A sailor lad on the ship, hearing the neighboring bells of Tintagel sounding out over the sea, thanked God for the favor that would soon bring them safe to port.

But the godless skipper told him to thank the steersman, the good ship and the ready sail. As if in answer to his blasphemy, the sea rose and the waves dashed the ship and its godless master on the rocks.

Now they say that the bells which went down with that ship may be heard above the surge of the ocean as it breaks on the iron cliffs, pealing out the invitation of the church, the invitation of God, the coming of death, and after death the judgment. For you today the bells of grace and mercy still peal and still ring. Not yet have they become a dirge or a knell.

Think of tomorrow! The road comes to an end. What then? Shall it be the end of the wicked and the unbeliever, which shall be cut off? Or shall the end of that man be peace? Can you say now, while still it is called today, and ere the night cometh, and before the road ends, "The end of that man is peace"?

Date Due